Presented To

_____

By

_____

Date

_____

Love's True Passion

LOUIS DEABREU

A WORD LOVE PRODUCTION

A poetic collection of love, identity, and Victory.

Love's True
Passion

Louis DeAbreu

Love's True Passion
Copyright © 2013, by Louis DeAbreu
Published by: Word Love Productions
Waldorf, Maryland 20603

ISBN 13: 978-0-9893352-0-1

DeAbreu, Louis
Love's True Passion / By Louis DeAbreu

Cover design by Emmanuel Barnes, 3G MediaWorks
Edited by Melanie Duppins

TABLE OF CONTENTS

About the Collection

A poetic devotional collection
To stimulate the soul.
When the cares of this world start closing in
And hope's light grows dim
We need words that stimulate,
Words to help us meditate,
Words that motivate and move us to always win.
We need "The WORD!"

Welcome to Love's True Passion:
An anointed inspirational word,
A better pill, forged from the open windows
Of God's manifested blessings,
That moves us beyond the expression
Of man's finite desires and into the realization
Of God's essence & true nature.

His heart's pleasure is to witness His true treasures
Experience the manifestation of destiny's measure.

LOVE'S BATTLE

Due to the nature of sin, true love is not free:
It's held bound in captivity.
Hostage to worldly perceptions,
Pretentions of finite men,
Leaning to their own interpretations
Of infinite divinity.
Left without the serendipity
Of love's true ability:
The gift that is free.
Yet freedom we fail to see.
No love, no purpose,
Just illusions of toil that produce no spoil
For men who coil in the dark,
Hoping for a spark,
A glimmer of boldness to set love free:
Take crucifixion down from trees
And live faithfully,
Instead of fearfully.

1 John 4:18

There is no fear in love [dread does not exist], but full-grown (complete, perfect) love turns fear out of doors and expels every trace of terror! For fear brings with it the thought of punishment and [so] he who is afraid has not reached the full maturity of love [is not yet grown into love's complete perfection].

COMMUNICATION

When climates change, the unprepared
Have no all-weather gear,
In tragedy, the tongue is bound:
Words fail to appear.

So emotions flare, then jealously enflames,
And confusion snarls and scratches at its cage.
The beast is unleashed. It's a killer and a thief.
In its wake, destruction abounds
Dancing to the sound of silent acquiescence.

Eminent domain is not established,
Relationships are ravaged.
Thoughts are negatively bombarded,
By the rust of broken trust.
Walls are erected; diplomacy rejected,
Misconceptions thrive.
Love is redacted, hope gasps to survive.

Lack of expression fuels depression,
Avoidance cuts a void, pressure peels to a chasm.
In disaster's turbulence, everything splits
In need of a mortar stronger than glue.
Through the ashes, we find a familiar clue:
No airplane, just a black box –
Evidence of a remedy,
A patch that was the necessity.

Exercise foresight and be on the watch to look [after one another], to see that no one falls back from and fails to secure God's grace (His unmerited favor and spiritual blessing), in order that no root of resentment (rancor, bitterness, or hatred) shoots forth and causes trouble and bitter torment, and the many become contaminated and defiled by it—

ALACRITY

I.

How diligently we work
To pay our cruel pockets –
Copiously toiling while internally boiling.
Steaming with resentment,
Evaporated contentment,
We plow on.

Futile tilling in infertile soil,
We watch our life's work & our best fruit spoil,
Not knowing why, we cry – each fallow paycheck,
Symptomatic of our spiritual neglect.

Empty inside, hungry for peace,
We pray somehow money will bring us relief.
Whether we seek health, love, or wealth
We learn wasted lives are our only return,
As we pour out our talents
Into broken cisterns.

II.

The ripple effect of poor choices,
Shows in our gaunt reflection.
Depths of despair eat our soul with infection.
A cavity of depravity leaves us weak and broken,
A shell of ourselves without a token.

Introspective revelation shows us our selfish nature;
Truth replaces our destructive deceptions.
We cling to the hope of redemption,
By caressing confession,
And rejecting all dependence on possessions.

III.

Thankful for Mercy, we digest Grace,
By Faith, we take our rightful place.
In God we truly trust:
We accept the inheritance of our Estates,
Soul winning is our mandate.

Colossians 3:23

Whatever may be your task, work at it heartily (from the soul), as [something done] for the Lord and not for men,

SWEET PROMISES OF INFIDELITY

Why did you buy the lie?
How could you claim to love me:
Display the outer appearance
Of covenant relationship with me;
State that you still love me –
Never left nor forsook me?

You fail to comprehend my hurt.
You deny you're dirt.
Everything you say starts with "I."

Only after you are finished pleasing yourself,
Do you make room for us!
I'm crushed!

From dust you came:
My love replaced your shame –
Filled every void.
Paid for your freedom,
with wages of Blood.

I AM!

I lay claim to you, my Love!
As we were wed,
When you said, "I do,"
I dedicated my life to you.

Have I not proven true?
Have I not provided for you?
Did you lack anything?
Was I not your everything?

So why would you decide to cheat on me?
Commit emotional adultery?
Choose a mockery, play with misery,
Become intimate with idolatry?
Why compartmentalize our love,
Adoring me privately,
Neglecting me publicly,
Wearing a cloak of hypocrisy?

You wanted acceleration,

So you chose an association
You thought would propel you faster than I could.
You believed their secret handshakes
Were the keys to revelation's gate.
You endured conditions,
For colors that would bring recognition.
Now, your entry into their jurisdiction,
Gives rise to a defeated enemy.

Without your permission he has no powers –
He operates in fiction, utilizing your diction,
To usurp your authority & nullify your destiny.
You joined forces with your worst enemy.
You wanted advancement; now they advance,
While you stay captive in a trance.

Failing to realize that I Am,
What always was, what will be:
All things point to me.

They have moved Me to jealousy with what is not God; they have angered Me with their idols. So I will move them to jealousy with those who are not a people; I will anger them with a foolish nation.

<u>PROPAGANDA</u>

You never made a move
Too politically correct
So you refuse to dance to the groove
Thinking is costly, causes intellectual turmoil
Going against the grain, 24 hours a day
Feels futile

If you read the Book you say you love
Your heart would still look the same
But renewing your mind
Requires unavailable time
Which is occupied pleading for change

The prince of the air
Has sown ample seed
Saturated the air
Now it's time to harvest
As his reign comes down
How profound
People look around

Wondering

Stating: what happened?

Still not moving

Just cycling old cycles of probability

In comes me

Standing

While you continually try to pull me down

Am I alone as I move beyond a bill fold

Please ask the Optometrist to open your eyes

See the war raging all around you

The fight is always on

You selfish pawn

Peculiar me confounded by your peculiarity

Displaying fruits of the spirit

All while my spirit is disturbed

As the insubordinate enemy dominates its

Subordinates

Who refuse to make waves

As "they" climb ladders

Playing political games

The enemy is aggressive
Strategically attacking the fringes
Amplifying the message on megaphones
Kids repeating songs of their own doom
Consumed
Watching shows in plain sight
Missing hidden agendas
We enjoy the show
Mesmerized by diversion
Anaesthetized as we swallow the pill
Sleeping with the enemy
While entertaining our own destruction

Psalms 14:1

The [empty-headed] fool has said in his heart, There is no God. They are corrupt, they have done abominable deeds; there is none that does good or right.

ANOMALY

I was not born in a manger,
Yet I was conceived in danger:
An affair that God's love did not share
Produced weeping and gnashing,
A family torn apart,
Now here I stand as the scar.
Born out of lust, I scream daily
GOD HELP US!
"Why me?" is my constant refrain.

Lord you are my strength;
I don't want to be sad anymore.
I've shed more tears that I can afford,
Sorrow has endured more than a night,
Weeping has plagued me all my life.
I need joy to come and shine its light;
For where I am weak your Joy shines bright.

2 Corinthians 12:9

But He said to me, My grace (My favor and loving-kindness and mercy) is enough for you [sufficient against any danger and enables you to bear the trouble manfully]; for My strength and power are made perfect (fulfilled and completed) and [b]show themselves most effective in [your] weakness. Therefore, I will all the more gladly glory in my weaknesses and infirmities, that the strength and power of Christ (the Messiah) may rest (yes, may pitch a tent over and dwell) upon me!

<u>YOU</u>

I.

No need for debate, you can rest your case
The preponderance of evidence justifies my faith
You've proven your truth –
That even a spiritually destitute prostitute,
The blackest sheep in a sullied flock –
Can be restored to their rightful place!

In my murkiest place, shadows dancing on my face,
I received unmerited favor,
Grace from my Fathers frock.
My lot was secured!

Before this moment, my life was a tomb:
Mired and cloaked in ignorance, consumed
In my own choices, I volunteered for doom.

I aimed to blend in
Like a world-class chameleon,
Wear their skin, speak their sin;
Self-destruct as I was programmed to do.

II.

I long to be just like them:

A reflection of humanity's tendency

To acquiesce to the demands of a few,

Drink from their cup of the devil's brew,

And purchase perversions and fallacies of truth.

So I surrender my power to an inferior

A shell with a poison interior:

A branch with no root in the tree of life,

I bud with bitterness and strife.

I place myself under their martial law,

Tolerate torture; rebel against only you.

To placate my foes, I gladly vacated my Throne.

With no control of my energy, I become a battery,

A power source of my enemy.

Mutiny!

I'm home, cowering – enslaved,

In my own trap, I have arrived:

I'm just like them!

Proverbs 29:25

The fear of human opinion disables;
trusting in GOD protects you from
that.

THE TRAP

If you are convicted, confined, and crushed
By the weight of your own opinions;
Desperate to be different, frustrated by failures,
Toiling for transformation, ignoring your need
For change within:
Your growth is impossible
Without improved choices, the only guarantee
In the cycle of life is death.

So stay the same, and, as life passes you by,
Wave hi to your grave of unrealized potential!
What was your destiny?
How will your purpose be measured?
Be sure to miss the blessings right in front of you,
As you continue to look in the rear view
At dream schemes.
See your minimized potential gauged
By people's perceptions; caught in a cycle
Of unlearned life lessons; doomed to repeat
The same class, all while holding the answer key

Or, you can challenge destiny's debacle!

The grave is not dug.

You are not yet food for shrubs,

So you can still decide

And grow to be the light that GOD shines through

Instead of the devil's tool.

Ephesians 4:18

Their moral understanding is darkened and their reasoning is beclouded. [They are] alienated (estranged, self-banished) from the life of God [with no share in it; this is] because of the ignorance (the want of knowledge and perception, the willful blindness) that is deep-seated in them, due to their hardness of heart [to the insensitiveness of their moral nature].

DYING DREAMS

How many graves will we dig,
Before someone decides to plant a seed?

The mirage of our needs crowds our hearts,
Like a forest of trees.

Until we stop being mesmerized by ourselves,
We won't start tilling fields and digging wells.

And feel the thrill of significance:
I think, I can, I will,
Moving beyond imagination and into creation.

When will we change our world and grow roots,
Produce mass fruit with tender care,
Cancel all fear?
When will we Arrest
Doubt & unbelief, the quiet thieves
Robbing us blind; killing our dreams?

Until then, we wish for the past

Remembering our friends,

Should and Would

Prefaced by I.

Until then, we find ourselves

Hiding our seeds,

Sealing our fates,

Speaking words that debilitate.

Negating all Faith,

Praying that the next grave,

Does not dig our coffin.

James 1:22

But be doers of the Word [obey the message], and not merely listeners to it, betraying yourselves [into deception by reasoning contrary to the Truth].

SURPRISE

Revelation has found me:
I'm ecstatic; I'm jubilant;
Sensory memory has me on cruise control.
I'm moving to my internal soundtrack,
The orchestra is conducted by the rhythm of my feet
As they hit the snare path.

I see symbols of bold feats; I'm euphoric,
Brimming with expectancy – I'm at peace.
I cast my cares as I say my prayers,
Ahead of me I see two or more
Gathered together,
They are singing a utopian score.
Worshiping in botanical garden splendor,
I truly surrender all.

Now I rest. I'm free!
Nothing here can harm me
I'm in a safe zone.

Beyond these doors, I'm a refugee
Refusing to allow the worlds wars to torture me.

No intermission.
As I take a deep breath, I look up
It's too late. I am flustered, in shock
Awed by Strife's thunder punch, I wobble.
I'm not dancing, I'm not drunk.
Now I'm out of control,
Trapped in the devil's foothold.

Isaiah 54:15

Behold, they may gather together and stir up strife, but it is not from Me. Whoever stirs up strife against you shall fall and surrender to you.

<u>RESENTMENT</u>

Truth isn't always a positive drug
It can be mustard gas to even the strongest of us

To peacemakers, it can be like an arsenic leak
That poisons in stages: day by day, week by week

It first strikes the tongue in a defensive frenzy
It responds to envy with an arrogant boast
Now comes an acerbic toast with bitter indignations

Glasses are raised to celebrate Strife's offense,
The invitations are sent.
Fear, doubt, & unbelief are the first to RSVP.

The time and place were set,
To wrestle the flesh to the death.
The autopsy will be inconclusive.

The subtle glove of circumstance
Left no DNA or traces of foul play
Just another life destroyed.

A family lamenting stolen joy
Calls for a Lobectomy,
In hopes of finding answers – someone to blame.

The results are in: un-forgiveness
And self-inflicted pain;
Anger that sticks like flypaper to guilt,
Chronic insensitivity piles up like silt.
Sadly they all willed to linger in hate,
And swallow condemnation's bait,
So poisoned relationships were their only fate.

Ephesians 4:26-27

"In your anger do not sin": Do not let the sun go down while you are still angry, and do not give the devil a foothold.

<u>REMEMBER</u>

I remember days of falling embers,
The sound of snap chasing crackle
While looking for pop
The overwhelming feeling of heat that's too hot
Like a volcanic eruption

I see sparks floating
Not fueled by timbers, yet they still explode
Exposed to my toxins, flames rise
I am the power source
This is not a fire shut up in my bones
Just resentment's reflection

A vague wish to backtrack to the beginning
Intervene; change the choices presently before me
I tried to smother them, stop them, and slow my fate
But it's too late
There is no rewind for a blaze that's burning

Looking for a way to undo the present,
I frantically scratch at the past
Looking for the point of origin
Where the spark took root

Thick black smoke clouds my view
So I can't see the present and choose
There is only now: eyes burning, soot smudging
The ripple effects affecting the nexus of time
I'm praying for inceptions intervention
Help; please don't leave me behind,
I'm alive
Forsaking my past I crawl to the exit and survive

Ecclesiastes 3:15

Whatever is has already been,
and what will be has been before;
and God will call the past to account.

<u>TIME</u>

Time waits for the dead
So that those who are alive can rise
Forsake compromise, dominate circumstances
Defeat poverty, overcome sickness
Each moment is an opportunity
It's decision time

All things are under your feet
Greater things shall we do
You are I AM
You can only be stopped
By what you succumb to
What you will accept
Are the things you'll possess

Is anything greater than God?
Time belongs to you, so wield it
Between two worlds we find you
It is what you say, what you do

Stop waiting, start doing

Its your time

Proverbs 12:24

The hand of the diligent will rule, but the slothful will be put to forced labor.

ROYALTY

If I could write better prose,
Then I would make allowances to take credit
For what I don't know, nor own.

Far be it for me to desire applause, no glory,
For when I take inventory
I find that the pros reveal the frailty of my con.

Please do not shower me with your love,
I am not worthy; I am only a humble servant,
Messenger, ambassador, and an emissary
All my power, right, privilege, authority is granted
By my Fathers diplomatic immunity.

With impunity I am made mighty,
I can pull down all strongholds;
By faith I can move mountains,
All so you can see His mercy enduring forever
As my beacon guides,
Shining the light on His Sovereignty,

Illuminating His exquisite majesty!

How wonderful is my Father: an eternal visionary,
He chose to love finite me,
Accepting me, even with all my contingencies and
unique fragilities.

But you are a chosen race, a royal priesthood, a dedicated nation; [God's] own purchased, special people, that you may set forth the wonderful deeds and display the virtues and perfections of Him Who called you out of darkness into His marvelous light.

FRIENDSHIP

Thank you for being a friend:
For taking your priceless time,
To help me find my value.

For giving me hope
When I could not cope.

Thank you for listening
Even when there was nothing to say.

Thank you for not leaving me alone
When Alone kept me company daily.

Thank you for trusting me
When your trust was not earned or warranted.

Thank you for allowing God to use you.
Thank you for answering the call to be a friend.

Therefore, I pray that this friendship shall never end
Thank you, my Friend!

I do not call you servants (slaves) any longer; for the servant does not know what his master is doing (working out). But I have called you My friends, because I have made known to you everything that I have heard from My Father. [I have revealed to you everything that I have learned from Him.]

SWEET DREAMS

Like honey, your nectar is sweet –
Caramel streams highlight every dream.
To wake would be a mistake
I am not willing to make.

You captivate me!

Velvet doubled as both texture and color,
Your promises made me melt.
Your flattery held me tight with all my might,
I could not take flight.
My future dreams are captive to my daily needs
No deeds were done, yet daily I watched
The setting of the sun,
Mornings rise witnessed no surprise.

The parable of sowers,
Found my grounds run down,
Entangled by overgrown shrubs.

I was looking for charms that were not frosted,
Hoping to find the end of never-ending rainbows.
The water for my good ground ceased to flow,
Trapped by the dam of my creation,
Desiring to cast down every thought,
Yet enjoying being stranded
In the land of fantasy.

Exalting escapisms' paradise,
Failing to rise,
Inflicting my own demise.

[Inasmuch as we] refute arguments and theories and reasoning's and every proud and lofty thing that sets itself up against the [true] knowledge of God; and we lead every thought and purpose away captive into the obedience of Christ (the Messiah, the Anointed One),

LOVE'S SPLENDOR

We have spent our days in pleasure;
Indulged in years of prosperity
Still each moment with you is without measure.
How could we explain what it is,
To bask in the glory of Heavens' splendor
Could we define with a poem's rhyme,
The look of your love
How Heaven has opened its windows,
Poured out its blessings
How every day
God helps us to make room
To receive the Grace, Mercy,
And fruits of the Spirit,
That He bestows upon us
Our cup overflows with your love,
The true love you continually show.
As every day you still say in word and deed,
That you desire to spend your life with us
Truly love does not fail!

All has been heard; the end of the matter is: Fear God [revere and worship Him, knowing that He is] and keep His commandments, for this is the whole of man [the full, original purpose of his creation, the object of God's providence, the root of character, the foundation of all happiness, the adjustment to all inharmonious circumstances and conditions under the sun] and the whole [duty] for every man.

THANKSGIVING

Lord, we want to give you more:
Slices of turkey will not be enough
To express our Love.
We want to give you our hearts.
There are so many unsaid words,
That never took form,
Left in the dark,
They can now find light,
Take flight on the wings,
Of true love's delight.

Thank you for your patience,
Support, dedication – for making us a success;
Your prayers took us through many tests,
So we can now find rest,
Knowing that truth is always best.

Our truth is that we're grateful,
That you are the depth and breadth
Of our desired very best.

It is truly a blessing,
To serve the one true King,
Living life upright,
As we continually seek Him.

Psalm 103:2

Bless (affectionately, gratefully praise) the Lord, O my soul, and forget not [one of] all His benefits—

HONEY

I am so thankful my love:
You are my sunshine, my moonlight,
You make the days and nights shine bright,
You are the mornings' warm dew,
The nights will never be lonely because of you.

How many lifetimes, have you been my lifeline?
How can I repay the debt?
Your love, your every breath,
Resuscitates and gives me depth.

I am so grateful that you chose to share your life,
Be my love, a true example of God's light.

1 Corinthians 13:8

*Love never fails [never fades out or
becomes obsolete or comes to an end]. As
for prophecy (the gift of interpreting the
divine will and purpose), it will be fulfilled
and pass away; as for tongues, they will be
destroyed and cease; as for knowledge, it
will pass away [it will lose its value and be
superseded by truth].*

HONOR & GLORY

Before my birth,
Before the foundations of the earth,
You believed in me, loved me, forgave me
Sacrificed your only Son to set me free
You offered me eternity.
Endowed with the power to crush principalities,
You gave me hope.
When life's vines choke, your grace is great,
Your mercy covers me unflinchingly.
You did not leave me,
Nor did you forsake me,
You gave me unmerited favor –
Blessings unconditionally
My cup overflowed,
Fear, doubt, and unbelief
Cower before me.
I am prodigally returning to Thee.
I come before your throne.
Thank you Father,
I am home.

Psalm 139:13

For You did form my inward parts; You did knit me together in my mother's womb.

THE RELATIONSHIP OF LOVE

"I love you" is not just a statement.

I want you to comprehend that while love is free,

Relationships cost more than pretty pennies.

Physical currency is not enough.

To afford this divine gift from above,

Love expressed through sacrifice,

The present is giving oneself

To a love that is beyond all else.

Relationship is the price of love's depth.

True love gives beyond any breath,

So today I give you me.

Praying while hoping for your reciprocity,

I lay my life down,

So that two may be joined to become one.

Tying a knot, that will not be unbound;

United by a greater, supreme love

That is not captive to legalistic shackles,

Man-made definitions,

In you I am forever vested.

We bear the unspoiled fruit

Of love's fruition.

My love, your presence

Is life's best present.

My only hope and desire

Is to be your gift,

The desire of your heart,

The answer to your prayers.

For it is undisputed, resolute

That in you I have found my good thing,

The answer to my prayers,

You are God's manifested Blessing.

Proverbs 5:15

Drink waters out of your own cistern [of a pure marriage relationship], and fresh running waters out of your own well.

__TEMPERATURE__

Where is the fire?

Tell me, where is the fire?

I see many sparks waiting to be flames.

I see friction's lonely stare,

Hoping to unite with His combustible heart,

So that they may blaze.

Still no flame - where is the fire?

Where is the desire

To put someone else above one's self?

To be obedient to our Father

Honor His desires, love Him

Seek Him diligently as a vital necessity?

So that we could comprehend,

The obligation to save the lost at all cost.

For at what price was your soul won?

At what price would you sell it?

If the gift of a priceless salvation was free,

Why don't you share it?

Is it not a talent?

A gift worth more than gold,

A gift so refined, it will never dull,

For its shine is sublime.

God's touch is not lukewarm.

The heavens blush,

As the open portals witness,

The Great Commission's Rush.

Revelation 3:16

So, because you are lukewarm and neither cold nor hot, I will spew you out of My mouth!

ROAR

No tiger, no lion
Can make the sound
Of a man who is truly found –
For when that man roars
He opens up doors,
Rips portals through time and space
That leads to his covenant place.

His roar is the transforming sequence,
That changes his environment.
He knows He stands between two worlds,
Possessing the ability to make his own keys.
Unstoppable, the new Samson,
That cannot, will not be bound.

He refuses to quit –
His plan is legit, his mane is untamed,
He desires to be what he is called to be.
Do what he was created to do,
Have victory, is the cry,

A roar so mighty that it resounds through time.

He knows he shall live not die,
So he sings many a sweet lullaby,
As he says goodbye,
To a world that could not stop,
The renewing of his mind.

Truly he is a devastator:
He takes territory
On the way to heavenly glory.
By grace he moves time and space
Roaring his way home
His echo resonates,
Clearing pathways,
Illuminating the narrow way,
He is not alone.
He leads his disciples' home,
Laying them before the throne.
He left no talents hid,
Presenting his gift to his father,
Mission complete.

Souls delivered.

He prospers with continual increase,
His roar intensifies,
It will never cease
As it is amplified at his Father's feet.
Well done was the only reward
Needed for such a son.

1 Samuel 17:47

And all this assembly shall know that the Lord saves not with sword and spear; for the battle is the Lord's, and He will give you into our hands

COMMODITIES

Priceless treasures lay bare their perplexities,
Find their conformity in simplicity.
Polar opposites find commonality
As wisdom is confounded by insanity.
Logic needs time to contemplate
How knowledge can liberate or debilitate;
How confusion can lead to clarity
If choice finds the right voice.
For guidance gives directions
That lead you to the right path
Or lead you astray.
Reward patiently awaits
Those who can find the narrow way.
Sadness and joy share an emotional connection;
Men deliberate destiny and seek purpose
While clinging to lifeless possessions.
A mate is found for the isolated,
The lonely discover they were never alone,
While realizing their void will not be filled

By the dust of more bones.

The rich and poor interchangeably occupy

The same time and space

There is a search for something new under the sun,

Only to find what the Son has already done.

Now bow down give Him glory and honor

For He has won and saved you from all

Conundrums.

James 1:17

Every good gift and every perfect (free, large, full) gift is from above; it comes down from the Father of all [that gives] light, in [the shining of] Whom there can be no variation [rising or setting] or shadow cast by His turning [as in an eclipse].

ON THE ROAD

On the road of death
Life intercepts
A man with no vision,
No wisdom, no knowledge,
Saddled down with debt.

He asks, "Whom do I owe?"
Collectors strike the hands out pose.
Is it me they are looking for?
Should I take this call?
Open their mail?
Am I in financial bondage here?

Total despair:
Spotlights dominated by fear;
Cries are drowned by tears!
Hope waits for federal notes to escape,
While praying for lower interest rates.
Loan quests are contingent on credit bets:
This is how we navigate the world's financial crest.

At its height, there is no bite,

But the systems' crumbling fast and falling forward;

Maybe is all the luxury they can afford.

For they lack the source:

No relationship; no access point; no reverence

That testifies to His supreme magnificence.

For whom He sets free is free indeed,

To access the heavenly account

That will never go defunct.

For its insured – a blood bought right

Whose price, no bailout could suffice.

Hosea 4:6

My people are destroyed for lack of knowledge; because you [the priestly nation] have rejected knowledge, I will also reject you that you shall be no priest to Me; seeing you have forgotten the law of your God, I will also forget your children.

DIVISION

We are made in His image
Individual pieces of the puzzle
Finite men seeking Infinite Divinity
Trying to unite to attain Serendipity
We stumble in the light
Fleeing for fear of the dark

At the core of our hearts
Failures' perfection tears up apart
So we partake of protection
Throw masquerade parties to hide our imperfections
Battling questions

Men litigate
In the end God deliberates

How many churches can we have on one block
Competing for members from next doors crack spot
The block is hot; every doctrine on fire
While souls continue to rot

They really don't want crack
Just compensating cause they can't find that Rock

Religion is the cry: we need more
But we can't agree on which text to follow more

Made in His image yet rotten to the core
Each one of us are pieces of HaShem
Selah

Oxymoronically, bonded free men
Could not perceive
That they were made righteous
Holy not because we love Him
But because He first Loved us
His Love is the key; take your rightful place
Enjoy your freedom, be whole
United as one in and through the Son.

JAMES 1:8

An indecisive man is unstable in all his ways.

THE CALL OF SACRIFICE

Mere words are insufficient to express our Love,
Actions augment our speech as we reach,
To be all that God has called us to be.

We shall help you build your house,
Fill it with God's best.
A token of our love and gratitude.
For dying daily on your knees,
So that your congregation can live free.

So we experience God's reality when you speak,
Feeding hungry children
Who excitingly await the outpouring of Blessings!

Jeremiah 3:15
And I will give you [spiritual] shepherds
after My own heart [in the final time],
who will feed you with knowledge and
understanding and judgment.

RAPTURED

Time goes by,

Still foresight has not left me blind.

Plainly I see all you do for me:

Compassion, consideration, communication,

How you vie for my devotion.

Searching for chances to sweep me off my feet,

Refusing to succumb to the entanglements of life.

You live free: facing all obstacles bravely,

Overcoming adversity. You do more than conquer:

You love me; truly adore me, open doors for me

That no one can shut.

Your splendor holds me: I am safe in the storm,

Protected in your arms.

Hold me, tell me, and show me what love can do,

As you war for me, Mighty Warrior of Love's truth.

Isaiah 45:3

*And I will give you the treasures of
darkness and hidden riches of secret places
that you may know that it is I, the Lord,
the God of Israel, Who calls you by your
name.*

WISDOM

The wise are not moved by circumstances:
They find opportunity in every situation.
The renewing of the mind attests to their mission,
Foresight grants them vision,
They know beyond a shadow of doubt,
That their foundation rests not in their wealth.
Confident in Him, they cast their cares,
Knowing He has proven reliable and trustworthy.
The Alpha, Omega – beginning and the end –
Above and beyond the constraints of time.
They know they will always win,
For time bows to Elohim's whim.

Proverbs 4:7

The beginning of Wisdom is: get Wisdom (skillful and godly Wisdom)! [For skillful and godly Wisdom is the principal thing.] And with all you have gotten, get understanding (discernment, comprehension, and interpretation).

VICTORY'S ROADMAP

We choose the weapons of our warfare wisely,
For they are not carnal but mighty.
So that we may pull down all strongholds,
As we put on the whole armor of God,
Knowing no soldier wars at his own expense.
For the price has been purchased
In Royal, Supernatural, Heavenly Blood.

We will not lose with the Faith we choose,
Fear, doubt and unbelief fall dead
At our beautifully shod feet.
Bound on earth and bound in Heaven,
Their ability to kill, steal and destroy
Has been rendered null and void.
Rebuked for our sake, the devourer has no case,
Now it's our turn to take our rightful place.

With his mighty Love, His grace covers us,
As we execute the rights and privileges
That God's victory secured for us.

John 10:10

The thief comes only in order to steal and kill and destroy. I came that they may have and enjoy life, and have it in abundance (to the full, till it overflows).

HEAVEN'S INVITE

Rise my love: today's splendor

Is a pleasure beyond measure!

As I behold your beauty,

Heavens inspiration pours out on me.

Visions of truth in timeless testimonies,

Attesting to the production of beautiful fruit.

With every move, you water good ground.

Your garden grows.

Sprouting seeds find their foothold.

This life has no toll: your love was purchased

With a priceless payment.

Destiny's alignment has led to this moment.

This day, I pray your hand in marriage

Please say yes! Allow Me

To bless this union, be the tie that binds

Our holy communion.

Will you marry me?

Malachi 2:16

For the Lord, the God of Israel, says: I hate divorce and marital separation and him who covers his garment [his wife] with violence. Therefore keep a watch upon your spirit [that it may be controlled by My Spirit], that you deal not treacherously and faithlessly [with your marriage mate].

STATUS REPORT

If we walk by sight, blindly,
The Great Commission looks bleak:
Like a thick smog sheet we're trapped in.
The saved have gotten lost in a fog
Of self-imposed depression, and spiritual recession.
The riptide of political correctness keeps it real.
Real quiet. Silently distances the gospel,
Keeps us in check. Speak and you'll regret,
Be blacklisted; won't be able to cash any checks.
Fear of being broke nullifies freedom,
Applying pressure to complacency's yoke,
As our souls turn blue and choke.
Real funny: we are the brunt of jokes
Let's keep it real, this isn't funny!
We complain about a lack of change,
Make excuses to recuse blame,
Court immobilizing shame, and feel weak.
Paralyzed by fear's glare, our tongues are snared,
Hooked to conformity, dreaming of liberty,
Wishing, praying, hoping that you would testify,

About the joy that is your strength.
Tell them about Love's True Passion,
Show compassion.

Romans 1:16

For I am not ashamed of the Gospel (good news) of Christ, for it is God's power working unto salvation [for deliverance from eternal death] to everyone who believes with a personal trust and a confident surrender and firm reliance, to the Jew first and also to the Greek,

IF

If and I were best friends:

We both thought this friendship would never end.

When you saw If, I was right around the bend,

The wonder twins!

We had each other's back:

"I wonder if" was our catch phrase,

"Inseparable" was our theme song.

Always played in the background.

"As if I did this"

"If I did that"

"If I would have"

"I loved to wonder if"…

If has a close relative, Wish

She fit right in.

"Now I only wish that"

"If I knew how I could"

Then I would be able to move beyond should

And do something, but only IF!

James 1:22

But be doers of the Word [obey the message], and not merely listeners to it, betraying yourselves [into deception by reasoning contrary to the Truth].

<u>THIRSTY</u>

Tears flowing …cares growing,

I'm running on empty.

There is nothing that I can actually see.

Where can I fill up a full cup?

I'm limp, impotently staggering, crawling,

I seek your glory; I dream I'm in your presence.

Is this a mirage, or truly the wellspring

Of your love?

I miss you: your essence is essential.

I'm thirsty – longing beyond explanation,

Panting exclamations.

All cried out and tired of doubt,

Sick of being fear's footstool, I bow.

Down I go.

Past my needs I hit the floor.

Surrender's nectar overtakes me, sudden and sweet,

You are the manna that makes me complete.

Jeremiah 2:13

*For My people have committed two evils:
they have forsaken Me, the Fountain of
living waters, and they have hewn for
themselves cisterns, broken cisterns which
cannot hold water.*

AXIOMATIC

Am I the sum of all the things I have done?

Does my past and present define my future outcome?

For what I once was, is no longer,

What I am provides ample evidence for conviction.

I am derelict in my duties,

Still sinning while changing.

Why would royalty want to redeem me? Claim me?

Are sanctity, redemption, reformation possible for me?

Righteousness has shielded me,

Right-standing has set me free.

Shed blood cleansed me, dignity clothed me.

The ultimate gift is my reality.

Axiomatically I wield power:

I have the right, the authority to take flight.

Here is where I discover my plight:

I define my father's abilities by my own contingencies.

I trust God solely as my genie in a bottle:

The answer to every wish, available upon my whim.

Can I dare believe, if it takes too long to receive,

If I sense delay in meeting my carnal needs?

My Father's desires for me are supernatural,

All I see is natural.

I think I'm serving God; He knows I'm just hustling.

My hands are not up, just out –

Waiting for my handout.

Payment for my servitude, the price of my obedience,

While Gratitude sits sullenly at a loss.

For words will not amply describe the thirst

Of the righteous who refuse to abide in God's word.

So all they see, seek, and hear is the death call of bread:

They answer to the very thing they dread.

Romans 4:3

For what does the Scripture say?
Abraham believed in (trusted in) God, and
it was credited to his account as
righteousness (right living and right
standing with God).

Galatians 3:11

Now it is evident that no person is
justified (declared righteous and brought
into right standing with God) through the
Law, for the Scripture says, The man in
right standing with God [the just, the
righteous] shall live by and out of faith
and he who through and by faith is
declared righteous and in right standing
with God shall live.

THE GIFT

Extra, extra!
Controversy sells, so I'm ringing bells!
Telling it beyond the mountain top,
I'm letting my words flow.
I'm going to drop platinum pop,
The weasel will be stopped.

What does this mean to you?
When was the last time you found
Honesty and truth?
All bad words have a root,
A cause that affects your tooth,
The ability to bite down and hold on.

Dawn's coming
You need to shower in introspection,
Wallow in peace,
Digest a gift that's not free:
Salvation. Its cost

Responsibility. I know,

What a dirty word!

But have you seen your reflection?

Lies attract flies, flies adore filth;

They gleefully gorge on sins guilt.

Don't worry, we know you're broke

Down looking for a palace,

But we offer more than a tow.

We got the ultimate hook up to go:

A free coupon with an unknown expiration date;

Your choice unlocks a gate – an eternal fate,

Choose quick, choose well: avoid the gates of hell.

What does it mean to be saved?

Do you know you are living in sin?

Would you willingly shackle yourself

When you have the keys to freedom?

Who else can share a life of clean air,

A sip of unpolluted living water?

Would you like to meet purpose?

Get a degree in unlocking potential?

These are all realities
Unleashed when you choose ME!
Who am I? Ask me, I'm waiting.
Just know this offer will expire,
Choose well.

Matthew 5:3

*Blessed (happy, blithesome, joyous,
spiritually prosperous— with life-joy and
satisfaction in God's favor and salvation,
regardless of their outward conditions) are
the meek (the mild, patient, long-
suffering), for they shall inherit the earth!*

TRUE IDENTITY IS FOUND IN JESUS CHRIST

If you do not yet know Jesus as your Lord and Savior, you have two choices. First, you can continue to search for your identity, seeking meaning and purpose. If you do, no matter how smart you are or how much you accomplish in life, your search will be in vain. Even the most successful man is only using a kernel of his potential if he hasn't allowed God to step in and expand his vision for who he is, and what his place is in the world.

On the other hand, you could realize today that a personal relationship with Jesus Christ is the key that unlocks your purpose and brings you into alignment with your potential. Simply by praying the below prayer, you can receive Jesus as your Lord and Savior, and enter an everlasting relationship of Truth:

Lord, You loved the world so much that You gave Your only begotten Son to die for our sins and whoever believes in Him will not perish but have eternal life. There is nothing we can do to earn this Love and there is no price that can be paid to gain salvation. I believe and confess with my mouth that Jesus Christ is Your Son, the Savior of the world. I believe He died on the cross for me and bore all of my sins, paying the price for them.

I believe in my heart that You raised Jesus from the dead and that He is alive today. I am a sinner and I am sorry for my sins and I ask You to forgive me. By faith I receive Jesus Christ now as my Lord and Savior. I believe that I am saved and will spend eternity with You! In Jesus' name, AMEN!

"**Relationship** is the price of love's depth. True love gives beyond any **breadth.** So *today,* I give you *me*."

When the cares of this world start closing in and hope's light grows dim, we need words that stimulate, words to help us meditate, words that motivate and move us to always win. Welcome to Love's True Passion.

In this his second poetry collection, Louis DeAbreu gives us a glimpse into a real walk with God. Go on this journey and see the passion of a loving father, as well as the trials of a wayward child trying to get back home. You will see that in the search for real identity comes the reality of VICTORY.

Word Love Productions
Waldorf, Maryland 20603

ISBN 13 978-0-9893352-0-1

NOTES

NOTES

NOTES

_____

_____

_____

_____

_____

_____

_____

_____

_____

_____

_____

_____

_____

_____

_____

_____

_____

NOTES

APPRECIATION

Thank you for taking your precious, priceless time to read this book. I am truly humbled, moreover blessed that you would participate in sharing Love's True Passion. It is my earnest prayer that you have enjoyed this journey and may you reap the fruit of its reward.